Love Always
Barbara

Bundle of Joy

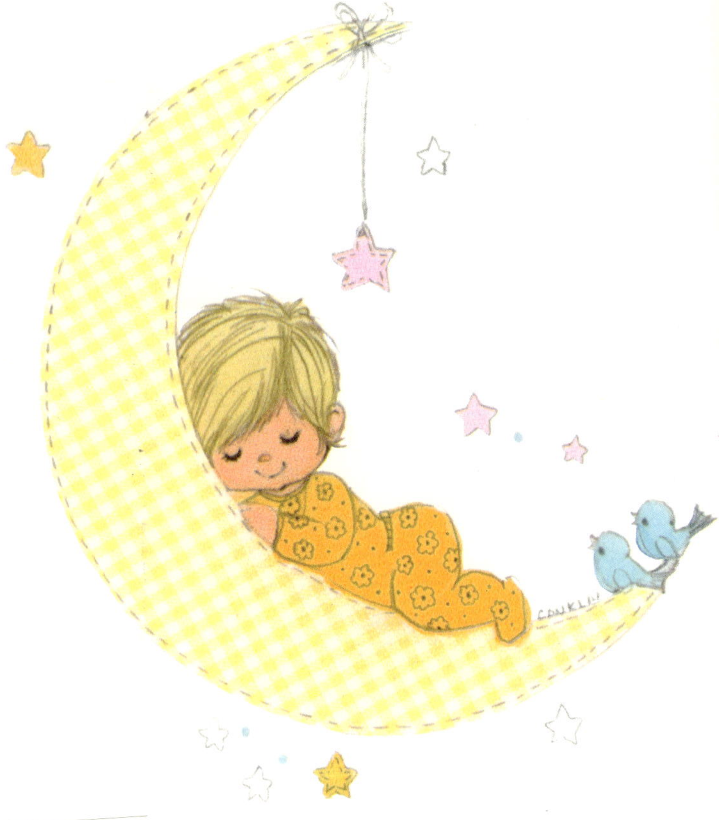
CONKLIN

BUNDLE OF JOY

Charming Writings About the Wonderful World of Babies

Edited by Kitty Clevenger
and Aileene Neighbors
Illustrated by Marilyn Conklin

♛

HALLMARK EDITIONS

"News to Cause Hysteria" and "A Waiting Room Grilling" from *How to Be a Father*, by Frank B. Gilbreth, Jr. Copyright © 1958 by Frank B. Gilbreth, Jr. Reprinted by permission of Thomas Y. Crowell Company, Inc., publishers. "Advice to Expectant Mamas" from "Tiny Garments" in *That's Me All Over* by Cornelia Otis Skinner. Copyright 1931, 1932 by Cornelia Otis Skinner Blodget. Reprinted by permission of Dodd, Mead & Company, Inc. "How to Deal With Bulky Contours" taken from "Mirror, Mirror on the Wall, I Don't Want to Hear One Word Out of You" by Jean Kerr. Copyright © 1960 by The Curtis Publishing Company. "If Your Last Name Is Pitt, Don't Name Her Olive" from *The Complete Mother* by Phyllis Diller. Copyright © 1969 by Phyllis Diller. "Stranger Than Fiction" from *Oops! Or, Life's Awful Moments* by Art Linkletter. Copyright © 1967 by Arthur G. Linkletter. All reprinted by permission of Doubleday & Company, Inc. "How to Hold a Baby" taken from "Child-Holding" from *My Ten Years in a Quandary* by Robert Benchley. Copyright, 1936 by Robert Benchley; renewed, 1964 by Gertrude Benchley. Reprinted by permission of Harper & Row, Publishers, Inc. "Reflections on Babies" and "Some of My Best Friends Are Children" from *Verses from 1929 On* by Ogden Nash. Copyright, 1933, by Ogden Nash. "A Baby's Back Makes a Good Mother" and "Just Money Will Be Lovely, Thanks" from *Special Delivery* by Shirley Jackson. Copyright © 1960 by Little, Brown Company (Inc.) All reprinted by permission of Little, Brown and Company. "Perfect Child Care" Copyright © 1957 by Elinor Goulding Smith from *The Complete Book of Absolutely Perfect Baby and Child Care*. Reprinted by permission of McIntosh and Otis, Inc. "This Bottle-Warming Business" by Bill Vaughan from *Sorry I Stirred It*. Copyright 1964. "Candid Camaraderie" by Margaret Fishback from *Look Who's a Mother*. Copyright 1945. Both reprinted by permission of Simon & Schuster. "Itchy-Kitchy-Koo" by Loyd Rosenfield from *Adam Had a Rib*. Copyright 1959, by Loyd Rosenfield. Reprinted by permission of Toni Strassman. "Such a Sweet-*Looking* Lamb" by Sara Lawson from *Home Life*, March 1969. © Copyright 1969, The Sunday School Board of the Southern Baptist Convention. All rights reserved. Used by permission. "The New Baby's Wardrobe" from *Stork Bites Man: What the Expectant Father May Expect* by Louis Pollock. Copyright 1945 by The World Publishing Company. Reprinted by permission of The World Publishing Company.

Copyright © 1971 by Hallmark Cards, Inc., Kansas City, Missouri. All Rights Reserved. Printed in the United States of America. Library of Congress Catalog Card Number: 75-126092. Standard Book Number: 87529-125-2.

BUNDLE OF JOY

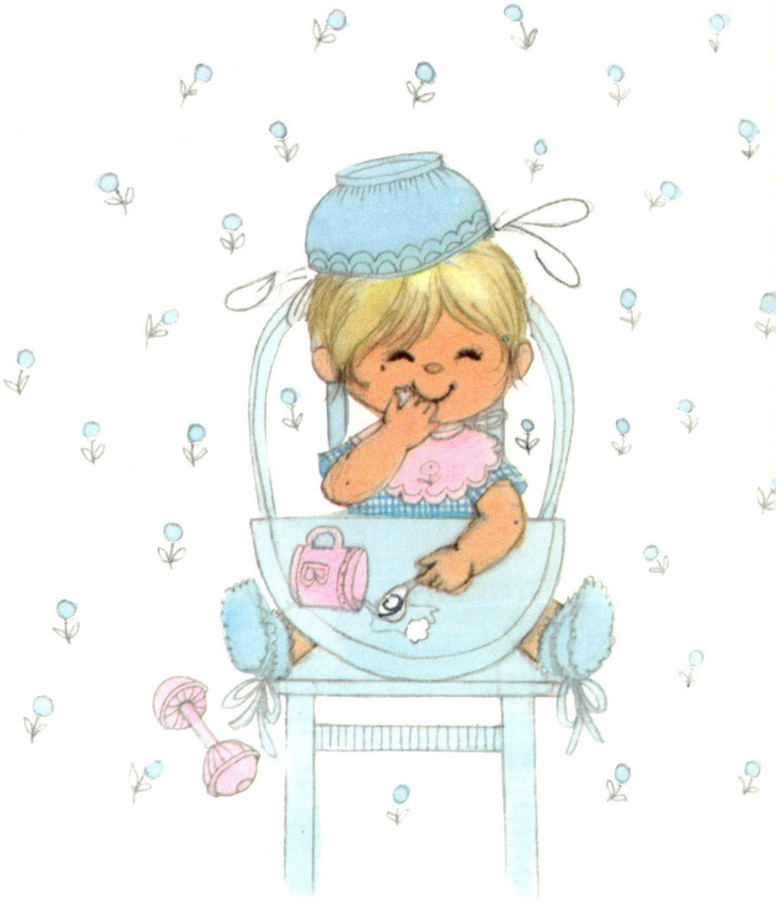

LOUIS POLLOCK:
THE NEW BABY'S WARDROBE

Before the blessed event takes place, it requires elaborate advance preparation, as author Louis Pollock points out in his book Stork Bites Man. *In this selection, he explains how he and his wife met the challenge, discovering that baby will never again in his life "be as well dressed":*

First we asked what was in store for us? The answer, obviously, was a baby. What is a baby? People have all sorts of opinions that might be used to answer this question. But, it must be admitted that, basically, a baby is an object.

Now objects, being material, require space. How much space? One thinks at first reasonably enough, that an area equal in cubic footage to the cubic footage of a baby, or say one little corner of your bedroom, would do for it. But actually no deduction more horribly wrong could ever be made.

The space which the baby itself occupies is the least of your worries. It is the space he doesn't occupy, but which is reserved for him anyway, that tends to crowd matters—at least if you live in a small apartment as we did.

First there is the bedroom. You allot space for the crib. Then there's a chest for the baby's things, part of which overflow into your clothes closet. . . . And the baby scale has to be put on top of something; usually either your wife's dresser or . . . well, why bandy words? A man can put his hair brushes anywhere. Mine fitted quite handily on the window sill.

In the kitchen there are shelves that must be set aside and prepared for the baby's bottles, bottle brushes, pans, sterilizing equipment, nipples, funnels, measuring glasses, formula, foods, etc. Later, when baby actually joins you, half the refrigerator goes over to him as well. This is when the formula bottles require the only tall space in the cooler which means, of course, no more bottles of your own on ice.

There remain only the living room and the bathroom, and they are divided equally. You get the living room and the baby gets the bathroom. No questions asked. None, that is, unless baby is not content with the bathinette, the special medications in the medicine chest and stuff hanging over the bathtub to dry, and decides that he desires a sunny corner of the living room in which to sleep....

You will find that you and your wife will spend a great deal of time privately discussing the baby. There is one routine that all first-time parents go through daily. It begins when the first baby garment is knitted or purchased. Your wife will show it to you and then lay it away—in our case in a cedar chest. Then the next article is obtained. Maybe this one is already in the chest when you come home. Off you march to inspect the little nightie, and, of course, to take a second look at the first garment you saw before. The procedure continues, item by item, as the wardrobe increases. You are taken to examine the last addition, and then, piece by piece (all carefully re-folded!) they are all reviewed and replaced in the chest.

Early in these pilgrimages I attempted to cut them short. After the first dozen undershirts or so I would try to maneuver so as to skip the rest of the stuff and return to my easy chair and paper. Somehow I never could accomplish this successfully. In fact the only change that did take place was in the other direction.

As the garments accumulated, the ritual became longer and longer and I finally started to brood over the extent of our offspring's wardrobe. At the time our baby was born I, personally, faced the world with two suits of clothing, a week's supply of linen and socks, an overcoat and topcoat of two and one year's use, respectively. My wardrobe had never run to greater lavishness than this. Influenced by such a background, it is only natural that I under-estimated the problem of clothing a baby. As a matter of fact, ours would have had to rely on just diapers and blankets had I superintended the outfitting job. But I lived to learn differently. The following will, therefore, be of interest to you.

There are shirts, dresses, and socks. There are night-sacks, sweaters, and booties. There are bonnets, buntings, and little kimonas. There are towels, washcloths, and bibs. There are crib blankets, carriage blankets, and receiving blankets. There are pillows, pillow cases, and slips. There are rubber sheets, rubber pants, and rubber pads.

And then there is the diaper—or I should say, diapers and diapers and diapers. I could go on, but the immensity of it all should be plain. Without wishing my child any ill luck, I sometimes think that the chances are he will never be as well dressed in his life as the day he was born.

ART LINKLETTER: STRANGER THAN FICTION

People are funny, especially when seen through the eyes of Art Linkletter. In this selection from his book Oops! Or, Life's Awful Moments, *he describes a humorous episode at the hospital:*

While visiting her father at the hospital, a lady whose dog was to have puppies that day called home to see what was happening. She was so excited to hear the dog was having a large litter, she told me, that she came running into the hospital lobby and yelled to the rest of the family, "She's had eight and there are more coming!" Heads swiveled around from all directions, and faces registered shocked disbelief. People were muttering, "Eight? Did she say eight?" and others were saying, "Yes! And more coming!" She was so flustered when she realized what the strangers were thinking that she announced, "I have to go back now to see how Daddy is doing."

SARA LAWSON:
(SUCH A SWEET-LOOKING LAMB)

In her article "Life With Baby," author Sara Lawson discusses some of the problems that the baby care books don't cover, discovering through humorous situations that experience is truly the best teacher:

Although I had read all available books on baby care, including the government's publication, I found there were far too many problems the books didn't cover.... One was how to wash an almost nonexistent neck surrounded by plump, shrugging shoulders and a double chin, said neck being the collection place for streams of sticky formula, orange juice, and strained foods. If we were stranded on a desert island, the cherub could have lived a day on the rations tucked away in the folds of her neck.

Nor did the books tell how to keep busy little fingers out of a mouth full of food. No sooner were the fingers thoroughly gooey with whatever was going down the hatch than they would find their way with the speed of lightning to (1) the feeder's clean clothes, (2) the feeder's hair, eyelashes, and nose, and (3) all furniture within reach.

I thought a plastic feeding smock with a catch-all pocket across the bottom would stop some of the identified flying objects. It did, especially rejected orange juice which remained in the pocket long enough for the busy little fingers to snatch the bottom of the smock, pull it up and pour the entire collection over herself.

Nor did the books help me with interpreting the bambino's repertoire of cries. These I learned quickly with practice. There was the "Curtain Raiser": A warning shriek of what was to happen if attention was not forthcoming. And there was the "guess-what-I've-done-again" yell, followed by a big smile while I worked with the safety pins and clean white squares. The "bring-on-the-food" order usually came when I was trying to finish another task before the feeding session.

It was hard to believe that such a sweet-looking lamb could be such a heartless slave-driver.

MARGARET FISHBACK: CANDID CAMARADERIE

I take his picture when he screams,
I snap him drooling in his dreams.
I shoot him gnawing at his feet—
That's known as making both ends meet.
I snap him in his epidermis,
As naked as an angleworm is.

I shoot him in his bassinet,
I shoot him dry, I shoot him wet.
I snap him when he crows and cries,
And when he registers surprise.
I shoot him wallowing in cereal—
That's when he looks his least ethereal.

And being human, I am glad
To share these pictures of the lad
With friends who try to pester me
With portraits of their progeny.
They whip theirs out with frantic vigor,
But I am quicker on the trigger.

CORNELIA OTIS SKINNER: ADVICE FOR EXPECTANT MAMAS

The subject of pregnancy's "do's and don't's" is dear to the hearts of most women. Famous actress and author Cornelia Otis Skinner discusses the confusion resulting from too many well-meaning advisors in this excerpt from her book That's Me All Over:

I have stated that the announcement of an expected offspring is the signal for one's friends to burst into unaccountable tears. It is likewise the signal for those friends and their friends and their friends' friends to come flocking like lodge members, bearing with them a mass of useless information, cheerful misinformation, and general confusion which they consider it their duty to impart to one.

Nothing is dearer to women than a nice long obstetrical chat. I have seen women who barely spoke to one another form life friendships over the comparison of their respective accouchements, and surely no topic is more absorbing to the feminine heart. I believe, however, that all such discussions should be confined to graduate mothers and old maids. For how any woman with a wide circle of helpful female friends produces a child without becoming neurasthenic for life is one of the miracles of Dame Nature, who, we are told, is herself a mother. So many and varied are the taboos and hazards of which her friends gratuitously inform the poor creature, everything she does is bound to be fatal, according to their composite advice, and her days are spent in a blur of bewilderment. People with whom she has had only a nodding acquaintance (and a pretty poor nod at that) rush up to her and beg her to confide in them, adding the cryptic remark, "You know, my child, I'm such a good friend of your mother's," which has always seemed to me to have doubtful bearing on the subject.

These prophetesses and soothsayers are divided unevenly into two groups. The Calamity-Janes, or disaster-foretellers are the larger and more upsetting. The lesser, but equally offensive are those noble, strident girls who think of themselves as fine mares, who have a baby as easily as one has a wisdom tooth and who harbor no tolerance for their weaker sisters. The first group come like the chorus of "Oedipus Rex," chanting of woe and disaster. They are the sad, tender women who visit one with pitying looks and solicitous gestures, who say with a shake of the head, "My dear, I know what you're going through" on days one is feeling extremely well and not going through anything in particular. They are the ones who say, "What! You're not wearing high heels!" While others exclaim, "You never should wear low heels!"—who inform you that what you're eating at the time might as well be prussic acid and who leap to draw up a chair or close a window with a wise look and a "My dear, you shouldn't." They have a happy faculty of inquiring who one's doctor is and, on being informed, exclaim with horror, "Not that man! Why he lost two cases last month." They are animated card catalogues of all the abnormal, disastrous, and fatal cases that have occurred in America during the last decade and when they leave, one retires to bed for the rest of the day.

The hearty pioneer women, on the contrary, are likely to call on days when one is feeling especially seedy and feeble. They are all health and sport shoes and think it nonsense one isn't out mowing the wheat. "Why," they say with scorn, "I swam the Channel the week before little Edward arrived." Or "We climbed the Matterhorn at dusk and next morning there lay baby Millicent on a bed of edelweiss!"

They go on the theory that what is good for the Italian peasant is good for all womankind and are firmly convinced they are the mothers of the race and that the rest of us should die off like weaker bacilli. In their presence one feels limp and inadequate and as if one's child might as well be the offspring of Ophelia.

To both groups the expectant mama listens avidly. In fact, with a first child she would listen to the advice of everyone from her maiden aunt to the Old Lady Who Lived in a Shoe. She feels somehow (and this a curious manifestation of the law of compensation) that she is the only woman of the century to have a baby and that America is awaiting the glad tidings much as Versailles awaited the arrival of a new little Bourbon. Her sense of importance increases in ascending ratio with her waistline; and that this also is a blessing. This is why she serenely believes the Fifth Avenue traffic is proud to halt while she climbs into a bus and why she is convinced (though few others may be) that she resembles Ceres or the figure of Fertility in Botticelli's Primavera when she is garbed in a jaunty little sports model, sleeveless and size forty.

And to me the most curious phase of all is that after it is all over—after our troubles, mental and physical, are at an end, and the author of them lying in the bassinet yelling its indignation over being alive—we sigh happily, act as if it has been a merry jest, and are quite ready to do it all over again.

NOVA TRIMBLE ASHLEY: WHEN A BABY BRUSHES UP ON YOUR HOUSEKEEPING

A creeping cherub can be trusted
To travel where you haven't dusted
As he investigates the floors,
Manipulating on all fours.
Behind the sofa, first, he goes
And gathers lint between his toes;
Then scoots beneath a Windsor chair
Where cobwebs dangle from his hair;
He crawls along a what-not shelf
And deftly finger-prints himself....
Try as you may, there is no stopping
A creeping moppet from dust-mopping.

LOYD ROSENFIELD: (ITCHY-KITCHY-KOO)

In his book Adam Had a Rib, *Loyd Rosenfield cleverly exposes the difficulty of conversing with and entertaining a baby. Here, he warns that if a parent asks his baby, "'Does um want a dwink of water?', the baby will eventually decide her name is Um...":*

Talking to a baby is difficult because you speak English and she (referring to our baby) doesn't. The baby doesn't know this. So far as she knows, you both speak the same language. For this reason it is ridiculous to talk baby-talk to a baby.

It isn't the baby who starts the baby-talk business; it's the parents. If a parent repeatedly questions "Does um want a dwink of water?" the baby will eventually decide her name is Um and that a glass of water is a dwink.

Baby talk seems to consist principally of inserting W's in words that don't have any, and removing them from words that do. For example, our daughter's name is Lisa, but my wife affectionately called her "Wisa." Hugging the baby, she was inclined to say, "Her so seet." What she meant, of course, was "She's so sweet.". . .

I was determined that by the time my daughter was one year old she would let us know she was thirsty at three a.m. by calling out clearly and distinctly, "Mother, drink! M-O-T-H-E-R."

Many visitors tend to rush up to a baby, yank it out of its crib, and go "itchy-kitchy-koo"—with one finger firmly pressing the infant's Adam's apple as if it were a front-doorbell. If the baby cries instead of laughing, the visitor drops the child distastefully and later criticizes it as being dumb and unfriendly.

I don't mean that a visitor should go up to a baby and say, "Good evening, miss," then solemnly shake hands. When you really wanted to make friends with my baby girl, you just walked over to her, handed her your gold watch and chain (or pearl necklace—she wasn't particular), and said, "Hello, there." She wouldn't reply, but she put on her best smile, gave your possessions the gum-and-saliva test, then hurled them across the crowded room. If you wanted to stay on her friendly side, you got them and brought them back to her. . . .

It was sometimes difficult to know what to say

to my baby when she was hungry and the bottle wasn't yet warm. But the topic of conversation wasn't really important, so long as a loud tone of voice attracted her attention from her own outraged wails. When the novelty of this wore off (in about 23 seconds) I tried the Gettysburg Address in low, somber tones. Novelty in the change in inflection reattracted her attention from her own throbbing innards. When her interest again waned I tried an imitation of Elvis Presley singing almost anything. When her sobs drowned this out I gave her the milk. Who ever heard of a little cool milk hurting a baby?

There is also a special way to talk to a baby who is happy and having a great time, but whom you want to put to bed so you can leave the house.

The first thing to remember is that the baby isn't interested in whether you get where you're going on time. So it is pointless to appeal to sympathy by smiling sweetly, saying "Bye-Bye" and attempting to sneak out. This will get you nothing but hysterics.

What you should do is flatter her. Babies, like people, love to be flattered. Bounce her up and down and tell her how beautiful she is. This will put her in a good mood. Put her down in her bed, but reappear almost instantly; then, while putting on your hat and coat, dance around her bed singing "Oh You Beautiful Doll." When you are ready to go, do a buck-and-wing dance out the door of her room. When you disappear, a howl of protest will begin. But before it can get well started, stick your head in the door and cry "Peekaboo!" This will delight her. She'll think it's a game. Slyly increase the intervals between re-appearances, crying "Peekaboo!" each time, until you feel you can get out of earshot before she realizes you are not coming back.

It may prick your conscience to employ little subterfuges of this kind, but they are the only way you have a chance. Besides, this is a good training for the future. If you think talking to an infant is tough, wait till yours begins to understand what you say!

SHIRLEY JACKSON:
(JUST MONEY WILL BE LOVELY, THANKS)

Baby gifts are always welcome but some can be impractical, asserts Shirley Jackson in her article "How to Parlay a Pink Elephant Into a Pair of Waterproof Pants":

The nicest thing about most baby gifts is the tissue paper they are wrapped in. Never throw this away. When the baby is a few weeks older and can lie on the bed for a few minutes to have his playtime, crumple the tissue paper into big loose balls and put it under his kicking feet. The agreeable noise will amuse him endlessly.

As far as the gifts themselves are concerned, it was very nice of all those people to send them, wasn't it? Write them polite letters. Say "Dear Aunt Sally, Thank you very much for the organdy dress. It will look darling on Harold when he is a little older." Say "Dear Mrs. Chandler, Thank you very much for the combination baby measuring spoon and safety pin holder. I am sure I will be using it every day." Say "Dear Dora,

Thanks to you and to all the girls in the office for the embroidered diapers. We will save them for best."

Write them all polite letters, and then put aside everything that is not absolutely returnable—like the pink beret your grandmother knitted with her own hands—and take everything else back to the store. Most stores gift-wrap baby presents beautifully, and make sure that the store name is included in the wrappings, so you will know where to take it back. And don't worry—they *expect* that the patented gadget for anchoring Baby to his carriage will be returned; any sales clerk will be able to tell you at once exactly what it is worth in undershirts and flannel blankets. It is perfectly possible that these gadgets are put into the stores merely to stimulate trade: the ornamental safety pin is displayed to catch the buyer looking for some useful and original gift and is almost certain to come unerringly back to the store later, bringing the new mother with it.

Some of the baby gifts you get may be useful. These come, almost without exception, from hard-bitten mothers who have been there ahead of you, and pass by without a second look the counters of lacy dresses and angora booties to see that you get a half a dozen cotton shirts, or a gross of safety pins. Furthermore, these true friends do not come over expecting to see the baby dressed in the cotton shirts they gave him; they can see the shirts hanging on the clothesline already, while the angora booties are safely on the closet shelf.

There is a certain type of giver to whom the fact of the gift is enough, without any reference to its practicality or desirability. These people know that they are expected to give the baby something, so they give the baby something. If the baby is born in the summer they will give him a winter bathrobe which will be full of moths by the time it is cold enough to wear it. If the baby is born in the winter they give him a pink sunsuit. It usually doesn't matter anyway, though, because everything they send is size 2. It is always very difficult to avoid thanking these people in the spirit in which the gift was sent ("It is more trouble for me to write this letter than it was for you to choose the gift—") and in general the trade-in value on such gifts is hardly worth the trouble of carrying them back to the store. If your baby is a girl, save them for doll clothes. There is a certain kind of doll, called "lifesize," which someone will give her when she is about six years old, which will be able to wear these clothes.

Most acceptable are the presents from relatives and close friends, who come right out and ask you what you would like them to give you. To them you can say, "Well, I have the baby's layette, thank you, but I would like a vacuum cleaner." Or "Baby won't need a single thing, because everyone's given us just loads of sweaters and stuff, but when I come home from the hospital I won't have a pair of shoes fit to put on." Or even "How terribly sweet of you to want to give us something! Just money will be lovely, thanks." One very practical gift, which people seldom think of unless it is pointed out to them, is a smoking hot dinner casserole—preferably chicken—delivered the evening of the day you come home from the hospital. Make sure you suggest this to someone who knows how to do these things right, with plenty of sour cream and mushrooms. Tell her to bring some French bread too.

People who give puppies or kittens as presents for a new baby need not be thanked.

JEAN KERR: HOW TO DEAL WITH BULKY CONTOURS

Many women worry about their appearance during pregnancy. Jean Kerr, in her book The Snake Has All the Lines, *offers a humorous, if not a practical, solution:*

Actually this is much simpler than it seems. The mother-to-be should get her hair set, apply a rosy-pink make-up, put on her most becoming maternity frock, and—here we get to the important part—climb into bed and pull the covers up under her arms. In this position she will feel chic. Overheated, perhaps, but chic.

ELINOR GOULDING SMITH: (PERFECT CHILD CARE)

To a new mother, caring for her baby can be an enlightening experience—traumatic, but enlightening. Elinor Goulding Smith relates some of these humorous (to others) episodes in her book The Complete Book of Absolutely Perfect Child Care:

The diaper, which is the most urgently needed article of apparel, is primarily a square or oblong of absorbent material which fits absolutely nothing. It is too small to be a sheet and too big to be a handkerchief. It is also too big to be a small baby's diaper and too small to be a big baby's diaper.

If you closely examine the shape of a diaper and the shape of a baby, you will find *no similarity whatsoever*. A person from another planet coming across a diaper for the first time would never in a million years guess its use.

Now for those who have never diapered a baby, here is how you do it. You spread out a clean diaper on a bed or table. Spread out a clean baby in his crib. Look at them both closely. Puzzling, isn't it? Fold the diaper sort of in thirds and then fold up one end of the now-folded-in-thirds diaper about one third of the way. Put it on the baby quickly, pin it wherever you can without sticking yourself, and then hastily hide the whole, ill-fitting thing with some sort of gown or wrapper or receiving blanket. (So that's what a receiving blanket is for.) (I've always wondered.) (I thought maybe it was for dressing up to receive visitors.)...

When the baby is still extremely young, he is cleaned by oiling him up well with a piece of absorbent cotton and some baby oil . . . But sooner or later, he is going to have to have a bath. In water. With soap. With a washcloth. In that folding tub you bought. That's what you bought it for. And this must somehow be accomplished without scalding him, freezing him, bruising him, drowning him, dropping him, breaking him, bumping him, frightening him, giving him pneumonia or getting soap in his eyes. However are you going to do it?

At this moment, if a grandmother, husband, sister-in-law or other callous intruder should arrive on the scene and laugh at your anxiety, pay no attention and go right on being as nervous as you like. The grandmother simply doesn't realize how fragile a baby is. Never mind that she bathed you. That's different. Besides, that was a long time ago, and it may have been sheer good luck that *you* didn't drown. Anyway, never mind how tough other babies are. This one isn't, and you must be extremely cautious.

When bathing a baby, there are two rules to remember. 1. Keep the baby's head above water at all times. 2. Be sure the pail is under the hose when emptying the bath. Failure to observe these rules is almost certain to result in trouble.

Most babies are fed about every three or four hours during the early weeks. Day *and* night. Night *and* day. Two o'clock in the morning for instance. Six o'clock in the morning too, for instance. And he can be very difficult about it. Sometimes the pediatrician says the baby needs to take five and a half ounces of milk and he'll only take four and a half. Then you have to stay up an extra hour or so, hoping that maybe he has a bubble and then he'll take one more ounce. You have got to get that one ounce into him at all costs, or he will die of starvation, or get rickets. Coax him, urge him, beg him, above all, pay no attention to your husband who is now standing around urging you to go back to bed and get some sleep. What does *he* know about babies?

If, after all your efforts, the baby absolutely refuses the rest of his milk, call the pediatrician. He'll be *glad* to chat with you at three o'clock in the morning. He was just sitting around with nothing to do anyway.

Presently, if the weather is fine and mild and the baby has obligingly gained some weight, the pediatrician will announce that you may now take him out for an airing in the carriage. However the pediatrician has no understanding of the problems involved. He has said you *may* take him out, but he has not explained when or how. After all, you can't jounce a baby around in a carriage too soon after he has eaten or he may "spit up." In a brand new infant, digestion is not always absolutely certain which direction it's going in, and "spitting up" is the euphemism describing the resulting confusion. Incidentally, baby raising is fraught with euphemisms like this which you might as well get used to. You can't wake him from a sound sleep to put on his sweaters, and you can't take him out before his feeding time or he may get hungry on the way.

The question is not *may* he be taken out, but rather, *can* he be taken out? Perhaps it would be best to wait. It's a little cool today anyway, and the wind is coming from the East. After all, there is *oxygen* in the house, isn't there? Open a window, and wait a month or so. No need to rush things. He'll have plenty of time for going out later on. He has his whole life in front of him. If you start letting him go out now, what will he have to look forward to when he's eighteen? Next thing he'll be wanting to smoke.

FRANK GILBRETH, JR.:
A WAITING ROOM GRILLING

The question most asked of "expectant" fathers by hospital personnel is "Would you rather have a boy or girl?" Giving a direct answer should be studiously avoided, writes Frank Gilbreth, Jr., in his aptly titled book How to Be a Father. *Here is his method of solving this ticklish problem:*

What sort of grilling will the father be subjected to when his time has come and he is led into the waiting room?

The question he will be asked the most often, by doctors and nurses, is whether he wants a son or a daughter. This line of interrogation, although sounding like harmless prattle, actually should be handled with great care.

An honest answer, for instance, might be that it doesn't make any difference to the father whether he gets a son or a daughter, as he would be delighted with either.

But look out! That sort of reply is certain to be twisted into indifference. And indifference is the basic trait of the villain, not the comic.

On the other hand, if the husband says he wants a daughter and he actually gets a son, or vice versa, he may also be in serious trouble. For the fact that he didn't get what he wanted will almost surely be interpreted as meaning that he didn't want what he *got*.

Of course there is about a fifty percent chance that the prospective father who says he wants a daughter—or a son—will be lucky enough to guess right. Those odds may appeal to the gambling instinct of many fathers. But if the father guesses right, he may be in an even worse pickle than if he had guessed wrong. That may sound paradoxical, but it just goes to illustrate how important it is for the husband to study all the angles.

Suppose, for instance, that the husband gambles and says he wants a daughter—and that he actually *gets* a daughter. Then he's stuck when his wife asserts:

"Yes, you kept saying you wanted a daughter. But that was just to hide your disappointment in case we should *have* a daughter. And now that our daughter's here, I know you're heartbroken because she's not a boy."

There are a number of variations to the basic question of whether the husband wants a son or a daughter. For example, the husband should beware of the shift nurse who, after getting no direct answer to that question, returns about fifteen minutes later and remarks casually:

"Well, you haven't told me yet what you think you'll name the baby. 'Junior'?"

Obviously, if the husband isn't on his toes, he will fall into the trap and give away whether he is hoping for a boy or a girl.

How, then, can a father-to-be evade questions from these would-be district attorneys? The answer, again, is simply by playing the fool, which, after all, is merely what is expected.

A moronic Mortimer Snerd type of laugh—awh-huh-huh-huh—is an extremely helpful stall, and if possible should be practiced by the husbands before the delivery.

Here are several typical questions, and some recommended answers:

Q. Well, Mr. Blank, are you hoping for a boy or girl?

A. A little of both, I guess. Awh-huh-huh-huh. Yes, I sure am.

Q. I guess you'd like to have a little boy, wouldn't you, Mr. Blank?

A. Do I get my choice? Awh-huh etc.

Q. I suppose you're praying for a son, aren't you?
A. To phrase a coin, "In God we trust." Awh-huh etc.

Q. Wouldn't you like to have a little girl you could cuddle?
A. Awh-huh etc. Thanks just the same, but I've been spoke for.

Q. No need to worry so, Mr. Blank. Don't you know we've never lost a father?
A. I don't think you ever even *had* a father. Awh-huh etc.

Q. Have you had any experience bathing little girls, Mr. Blank?
A. No, Honey, I guess you'll have to get help from somebody else. Awh-huh etc.

When not replying in idiotic fashion to these probing personal questions and similar intrusions, the husband should pace the waiting room while twisting his hat in his hands and wearing the most worried look he can muster. Also, if he wants to cooperate and provide a real *hearty* laugh, he should mutter from time to time: "If only my sainted father had told me the *truth* about all this, I'd never have even gone *near* a woman, let alone *married* one."...

If the husband concentrates on playing the fool,

thus spreading joy over the hospital grapevine to hundreds of otherwise grim faces, the time will pass swiftly. Almost before he knows it, a nurse will be telling him that he is the father of a fine, bouncing baby.

OGDEN NASH: REFLECTION ON BABIES

A bit of talcum
Is always walcum.

KATHERINE DAVIS: WHAT IS A BABY?

A baby's a sigh
And a gurgle and coo,
A bundle in a blanket
Of pink or of blue—
A baby's a mouth
That is tiny and rosy,
Eyes that are frequently
Just a bit doze-y,
A small tuft of hair
And a sleepy-time air . . .
A baby's the center
Of talcum and rattles,
Safety pins, booties, and noise,
Bottles and formulas,
Diapers and blankets
And all kinds of cuddly toys . . .
A baby's a wonderful
Joy and delight,
Who sees that you walk the floor
Night after night,
A pleasure, a treasure,
A dream that's come true . . .
A baby is joy
And much happiness, too!

LOUISE HAJEK:
JUST DESSERTS

Baby dear is cushion-plump
He finds all food is sweet
Fruits and milk and cereal,
Each one is a treat.

How swiftly he dispatches all,
Then blissfully he lingers
On the best of all desserts,
Those delicious fingers.

BILL VAUGHAN:
(THIS BOTTLE-WARMING BUSINESS)

Newspaper columnist Bill Vaughan has great respect for fathers who have helped with the 2 a.m. feeding. He should know. He's been there, as he confesses in this selection from his book Sorry I Stirred It:

All right, so they have done this research which indicates that the average baby doesn't care whether the milk is warm or cold, just so it's milk. The result has been a loud outcry from people, and even fathers, who have been up in the late and early hours heating the formula, and now they feel that science, which thought up this bottle-warming business in the first place, should reimburse them for the wasted time.

I would like to demur. I have served my stretch of fumbling around in the lonely hours of the night and heating the bottle in the pan of water (before the era of the individual electric bottle warmer this was, young folks) and squirting it on the inside of the wrist.

It did me a world of good. An entire world.

I am a better man for it. This country was built by men (and an occasional woman) who heated up the 2 A.M. bottle. The mistake of the researchers at Bellevue Hospital, whence this report emanates, is that they are thinking only of the baby. They say the baby would as soon have the milk cold.

But we must all understand that the object of proper baby care is not, ultimately, the welfare of the baby. Although it should be taken into consideration. The idea is to break the spirit of the father.

Surely I don't mean "break." Gentle is a better word, or temper, or refine.

The men who today are making the decisions about Cuba, about Vietnam, about space travel, learned more about patience, about understanding, about tolerance, while getting the baby's bottle to the right temperature and into the baby, than they ever learned at Harvard or Southeast Oklahoma Teachers.

The main purpose of the baby is to educate the father. Pediatricians understand this. If the child is ill they give instructions that two of the green pills should be given every 37 minutes and one of the red pills every two hours. The regimen does not injure the baby and does wonders for the father.

It gives him a feeling of importance. It salves his ego. If he cannot go out and protect the baby from bands of hostiles and packs of wolves, he can at least remember which pills are which, and keep track of what time they are to be ingested.

I shudder to think what kind of world we are going to have if bottles are no longer heated. The babies may be O.K. But the fathers will not have had the enriching experience of padding around the kitchen and examining the bedrock questions of their lives, such as "How did I get into this mess?"

Fathers who have heated bottles have learned a lot. They have learned compassion. They have learned to lie a little, as when they say, "All right, Sam, it's warm enough now," when it isn't.

If a man does not come to grips with himself at the darkest hour of the morning, when life is at its lowest ebb, and he is standing with one bare foot on the cold linoleum and the other on the windowsill as he smokes a solitary cigarette and looks out at the stars while waiting for the milk to warm, then he will never come to grips with anything in this life.

Now, at this crucial moment in our history, we are told that the temperature of the milk doesn't matter. I doubt the wisdom of making this public. Suppose that it doesn't really affect the health of our infants, we are still paying a high price if we lose an entire generation of fathers.

OGDEN NASH: SOME OF MY BEST FRIENDS ARE CHILDREN

Ichneumons are fond of little ichneumons,
And lions of little lions,
But I am not fond of little humans;
I do not believe in scions.

Of course there's always our child,
But our child is different,
Our child appeals
To the cultivated mind.
Ours is a lady;
Boys are odoriferant;
Ladies are the sweetness;
Boys are the rind.

Whenever whimsy collides with whimsy
As parents compare their cherubs,
At the slightest excuse, however flimsy,
I fold my tent like the Arabs.

Of course there's always our child,
But our child is charminger,
Our child's eyes
Are a special kind of blue;
Our child's smile
Is quite a lot disarminger;
Our child's tooth
Is very nearly through.

Mankind, I consider, attained its zenith
The day it achieved the adult;
When the conversation to infants leaneth,
My horse is bridled and saddult.

Of course there's always our child,
But our child is wittier;
Our child's noises
Are the nicest kind of noise;

*She has no beard
Like Tennyson or Whittier;
But Tennyson and Whittier
Began as little boys.*

*The Politician, the Parent, the Preacher,
Were each of them once a kiddie.
The child is indeed a talented creature.
Do I want one? Heaven forbidde!*

*Of course there's always our child
But our child's adorable.
Our child's an angel
Fairer than the flowers;
Our child fascinates
One who's rather borable;
And incidentally,
Our child is ours.*

SHIRLEY JACKSON: A BABY'S BACK MAKES A GOOD MOTHER

A sense of accomplishment is important to a new mother, asserts Shirley Jackson. In her article "Cleverest Man," she illustrates the pride that only a successful mother can feel:

Probably the cleverest man I have ever known was the pediatrician who took care of my oldest child some fifteen years ago. When Laurie was about three months old, and in for his regular checkup, the doctor answered all my silly questions and soothed all my nervous doubts, solved my imaginary fears, and reassured me patiently. Finally he sat Laurie neatly on the examination table, holding him with one hand, and with the other hand he patted the middle of Laurie's small back. "This boy has a fine straight back," the doctor said. "A fine straight back. You've done a *very* good job with him."

It was the most wonderful thing I had ever heard. Glowing, excited, secretly nominating myself for Mother of the Year, I hurried Laurie home in his carriage: I could hardly wait to call my husband at his office and tell him we had built Laurie's back nice and straight. I called my mother and my mother-in-law and told them that Laurie's back was unusually straight, and both of them congratulated me soberly. I told my neighbors what *my* doctor had said about *my* baby and was only prevented by natural reticence from giving out general advice on care and feeding, and particular advice on straight backs. Here I had thought all along that I was doing everything so clumsily and so amateurishly; I would have put myself very low on the maternal scale; I was jealous of the competence my neighbors seemed to show, and yet all the time I had been—instinctively, I admit, but that made it even more gratifying—doing just the right things, and the proof of it was there: Laurie's back was nice and straight.

So is every baby's.

FRANK GILBRETH, JR.: NEWS TO CAUSE HYSTERIA

A TOOTH, A TOOTH! Baby's first tooth and mother's subsequent exultation prompts author Frank Gilbreth, Jr. to consider this universal phenomenon. Here he advises dad on how to handle the potentially explosive announcement:

There is nothing particularly remarkable about producing teeth. All normal babies—and many animals—get them. The process is slow and sure, and completely routine from a biological standpoint.

Even so, the emergence of the baby's first tooth is almost always greeted by the mother as a minor miracle and an occasion for rejoicing. Although the baby couldn't have held back the tooth if it had tried, the mother still heaps extravagant praise on the little creature for a splendid job, well done.

Long before the first tooth arrives, it is used in absentia as an excuse for any bad habits which the baby may develop.

"The poor little thing is teething," the mother explains to the father, to visitors, and to neighbors when the baby cries, spits up, sulks, won't eat, or won't go to sleep.

Since children teethe off and on right up until they're full grown and get their wisdom teeth, this alibi can be carried to ridiculous extremes and used to excuse everything from thumb sucking to smoking marijuana.

But the important thing for the father to remember is that the first tooth, which originally lifts his wife to the peaks, may also plunge her quickly to the depths. The father should not let any of this upset him, since it is a routine occurrence and will blow over soon enough. He should just try . . . to match his wife's mood.

Conveniently, the first tooth usually makes its appearance right up front. The mother, who knows exactly where to look for it, almost invariably is its discoverer.

"Come quick, come quick," she probably will call excitedly to her husband, who may be taking a shower, talking to his boss over the telephone, or trying to get a few winks of much-needed sleep. "Quick, quick, quick!"

With his heart in his throat, the husband leaps naked from the shower, slams down the telephone, or hurls himself out of bed, as the case may be, and arrives on the dead run at the nursery. He's greatly relieved to note that, at any rate, the baby still hasn't turned blue.

"What in God's name is the matter?" he inquires fearfully.

"A tooth, a tooth," she whinnies gleefully. "I saw it. I felt it. A tooth! The baby has a *tooth.*"

This may not seem important enough news to cause hysteria. However, the father is likely to bring the roof down on his head if he inquires, "So what?" or if he remarks that he can't get too excited, since he himself has more than a score of teeth. The recommended procedure is for the husband to drape a diaper or something around himself, if he has been summoned dripping from the shower, and to ejaculate:

"A tooth? Did you say a tooth? No kidding, not a *tooth!*"

"Yes," his wife affirms gloatingly. " A *tooth.* I saw it and I felt it."

There may be a temptation here for the husband to ask whether she remembered to boil her finger for twenty minutes before she put it in the baby's mouth. But he should cast aside the temptation and continue to play up to her good humor, which will be short-lived in any event.

"Goodness gracious me," he stalls. "What do you know about that! A *tooth*. Where? Let me see. Open your mouth, Little Precious, and let Daddy see."

Of course the surest way to make a baby act as if it had lockjaw is to indicate that it should open its mouth. The way to examine a baby's teeth is to make believe that you are examining its toes or fingers—and wait until it yawns, laughs, or cries.

And although the mother may occasionally sneak her own finger into the baby's mouth, she has no intention of allowing the father to do so now. Consequently, for the time being Poppa will have to content himself with a minute and repetitious description of the tooth, as furnished by his wife.

"It's right about here," she says, pointing to her own mouth. "Yes, that's exactly it—right about here."

"And exactly what does it look like?" he stooges.

"Small and white and sharp on the end. And only a little bit of it showing right now. Hardly any more than a teeny bit."

"Well I'll be darned. No kidding. Small and white, eh?"

"Yes, small and white and very cute and . . ."

And now her mood may suddenly change from elation to dejection. But there is nothing the husband can do about this.

"It's so sad, in a way," she says. "It's a cute little tooth. Mighty cute little tooth. But . . ."

"What's sad about a tooth—unless it has to be

filled or something?" the husband wants to know.

"Well, just think, we don't have a *real little* baby any more. When a baby has teeth—even one tooth—it's not a real *little* baby any more. Our *little* baby is, well, growing up. In fact..."

"Don't get yourself upset now, dear," the husband begs.

"I'm not upset," she chokes. "But our *little* baby is gone—gone forever; gone *forever*."

ROBERT BENCHLEY: HOW TO HOLD A BABY

Humorist Robert Benchley, who delighted readers of The New Yorker *magazine for many years, also wrote a number of books that captivated an even larger audience. In this selection from* My Ten Years in a Quandary, *he advises "male relatives who find it necessary for one reason or another to hold a baby ...":*

Fathers, godfathers and uncles will be glad to learn that baby specialists have now decided that the child is given beneficial exercise by being shifted about from one position to another in the holder's arms. This will eliminate a great many dirty looks and much kidding at the male relative's expense.

No male relative, in his right mind, ever takes a baby to hold of his own free will. The very thought of dropping it, a thought which is always present, is enough to reduce all his vital organs to gelatin. Some female always suggests it. "Let Joe hold him for a minute. Hold him, Joe!"

So, Joe, sweating profusely, picks the infant up

and becomes a figure of fun. "Look at how Joe's holding him, Bessie! Like he was a golf bag!" "Poor kid—put him down, Joe!" "Look out, Joe,—you'll strangle him!" Lynching is on in the air. But now Joe can come back with the excuse that he is giving the baby exercise. "You women hold him in that one position all the time, and his body doesn't develop symmetrically. Ask anyone who knows!"

For male relatives who find it necessary for one reason or another to hold a baby, the following positions are suggested as being most beneficial to the child's development and most conducive of apprehension on the mother's part.

If the child has to be lifted from its crib by the father or uncle, the old-fashioned way of reaching down and grabbing it under the arms should be discarded. The male relative should get into the crib with the child, and lie on his back (his own back), taking the child on his chest and rising to a sitting posture. Then call for someone else to come and lift both father and child from the crib at once.

In taking the baby from the arms of someone else, as at the christening or general family gathering, grasp one of the child's ankles firmly in the right hand and tell the other person to let go. The child will then swing, head down, from the other person's arms, and can be twirled in a semi-circle, in the manner of an adagio dancer, until the arc is completed, and the child lands across the uncle's shoulder, the latter, if possible, still holding firmly onto the ankle. This will develop the child's leg, and give it poise.

A still better way to develop the child is to have *it* hold the male relative.

PHYLLIS DILLER:
IF YOUR LAST NAME IS PITT,
DON'T NAME HER OLIVE

Among the many approaches to choosing a name for baby, Phyllis Diller selects rather unusual criteria. In her book The Complete Mother, *she writes "There are lots of Bobs and Bills but only one Samovar":*

Be very careful to select a name your child will be happy about. There are lots of Bobs and Bills but only one Samovar....

1. Make the name simple, not like our neighbor's child, Bartholomew, who was held back in first grade because he couldn't spell his name.
2. Give your son a common name—one that when it is yelled out by the teacher doesn't quite so definitely establish who it is.
3. Give your daughter an unbelievably homely name so that young men chase her because they think she's named for someone who is going to leave her money....

If your last name is	don't call her
Pad	Lily
Bopper	Teenie
Carr	Kitty
Keene	Peachie
Cohen	Vanella
Pitt	Olive
O'Graph	Mimi
If your last name is	don't call him
Vale	Noah
Furter	Frank
Labor	Manual
Waggon	Chuck
Walk	Jay
Horn	Otto
Quido	Amos

MARJORIE HARRIS: AREN'T BABIES GRAND

*They don't have any teeth
And they don't have much hair,
They can't talk at all,
They can't walk anywhere,
They sleep all day long
And stay up the whole night,
They yell every time
Things don't suit them just right;
But with all of the worry
They cause you, by heck,
They do make a home—
(Yeah, they make it a wreck)
And they make you so happy,
So proud and so glad—
Isn't it wonderful
Being mother and dad?*

Set at The Castle Press in Intertype Walbaum, a light, open typeface designed by Justus Erich Walbaum (1768-1839), who was a type founder at Goslar and at Weimar. Printed on Hallmark Eggshell Book paper.

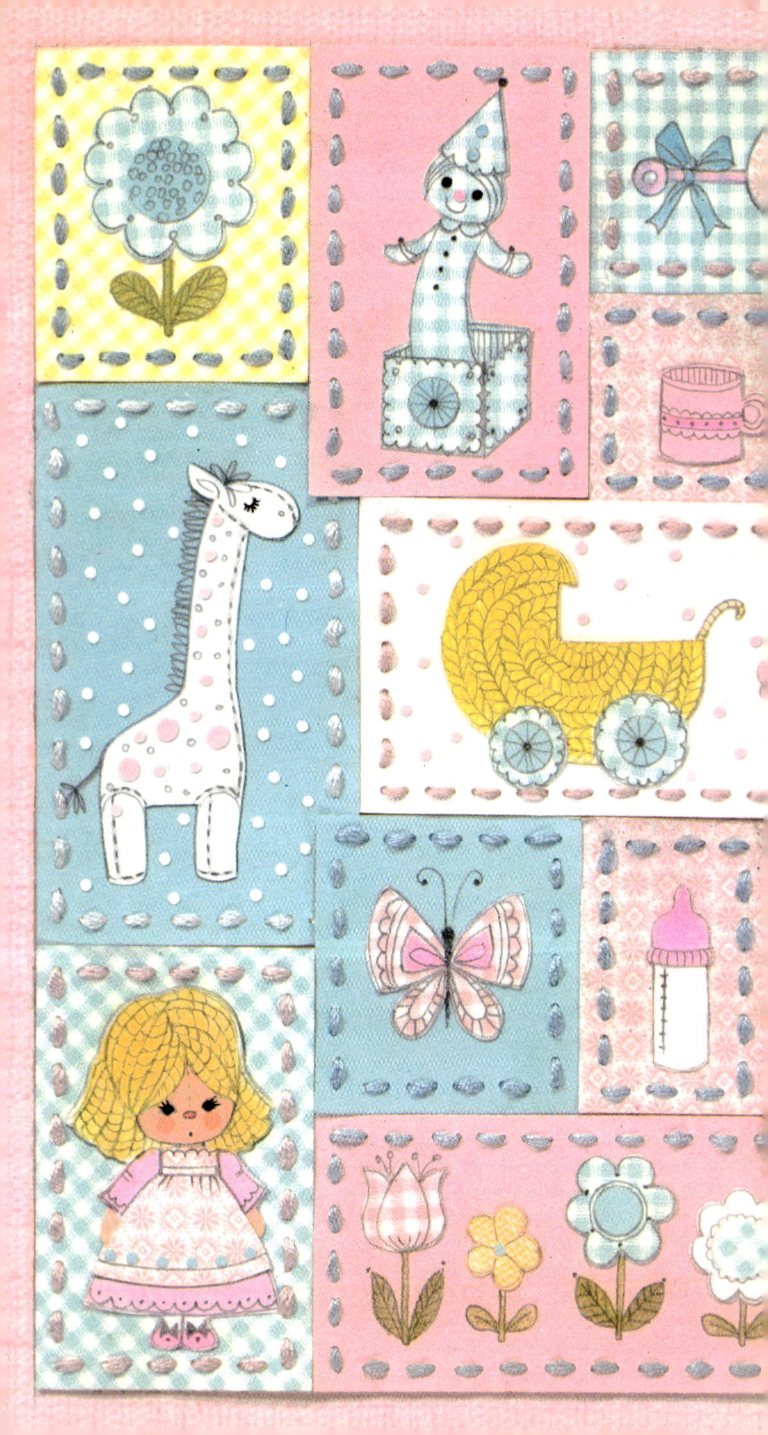